WEAVING OUR BASKETS OF LIFE

POEMS AND OTHERS

By

Patrice Musa Ngantu

Judith Kome Ngantu

First Published in 2023

Miraclaire Publishing
Kansas City, MO 64133, USA
www.miraclairepublishing.com / info@miraclairepublishing.com

ISBN: 978-1-954154-19-3

CONTENTS

Part I: Life by Patrice Musa Ngantu 5

Dream: Stagnant Progress /Vain Labour) 7
Failure: (Dream) Failing where others easy success find 8
Man and Natural Elements (bid their time) 10
All is Vanity 11
A Prayer 12
Decide the Part to Play (1) 13
Decide the Part to Play (2) 15
Be Ware 17
Racial Conflicts 18
Mutual Respect 19
The Missing Link 20
Butchering the dead 22
Food for Thought 23
The Real Thing (On Death of Father) 24
Philosophical 25
Missing Facts 27
Sun-set in Cameroon? 29
The Big Question (on millipedes copulating) 32
Hurrah to ideologies! When shall it come? 34
Concrete Time 36
The Phoenix personified? 38
Small No Be Sick 39
More questions: What future? 42
What Difference? 43
New Year Morning 44
Communion: Old and Young 45
Practically Philosophical 46

Part II: Many Hearts, Many Voices by Judith Kome Ngantu **47**

My Redeemer 49
My Baby 50
Queen of the Night 51
The Widow 52
Desperation 53
Love Lessons 54
You once were mine 55
Dilemma 56
The Sermon 57
Life 58
Again 59
It hurts at night 60
Woman-man 61
Cassanova 62
Red Eyes 63
Mama 64
Beauty Technology 65
Virtues 66
My African Man 67
My flower pot 68
No Promises 69
Good women 70
Proverbs 71
A Pastor's tears 72
We age 73
Vanity 74
Tears of a Bastard 75

Part I: Life

by

Patrice Musa Ngantu

Dream: Stagnant Progress /Vain Labour)

My affairs in order
I my physical mass
On its physical bed
Abandon
    And my mind's eye on a trip over the expanse
of my acquaintances
    Took
    In search for a conveyance to the Unknown
...
    Land of Peace!
    We from one end to the other
    Roamed.
    In vain did we our globe
    Try to intercept
    The fault?
    My companions!
    -always distracting me to what we'd left
    Behind.
And then when we'd the goal reached
In so short the twinkling of an eye
We could not the START from the FIN distinguish,
And wondered if we'd anywhere else been.
    (20/06/77)

Failure: (Dream) Failing where others easy success find

All before me is clear.
My friends with ease
Have the entire wall climbed:
In view can none other be seen.

But close at my heels impatiently
Are others scampering
My clearance awaiting.
No step backwards else
The living stone does break a- tumbling down.
No step forward for
My vein-swollen hands and feet
DO tears of fear shed
And shakily cower from
That daring Venture.

All before is clear
And the throng behind me press ….
I the goal do touch …. And yet so far does it feel!
Would there were one
To stop and me hull over!

Shakily do I at the line stand
No step forward,
And yet none backward able!
A lose of foot-hold?
A loosening of grip?
And we are all set to toppling down.

Oh wretched me,
Failing where others easy success find!
And to my success are all eyes
With expectations turned!

Man and Natural Elements (bid their time)

The day into darkness and unto day opens
Just when our saturation for one would to hate turn.
Thus, in black and in white do we in alternation
bathe
To curb boredom, as in a child-and-toys syndrome

When, fearing another flood Creation begins to
weep,
The sun down on her does smile
And her tears dry away.
The smile turned to laughter soon the cheeks too dry
makes.

When up comes a cry of despair and longing for a
"Cooling"
Then the sun, dark-browed
Would behind the black clouds withdraw
For heaven to unleash big tears of despair
Onto the patched earth ere it cracks to dearth.

The patient impatient sun with a knowing smile
Bids its time….
He will always have his say!

All is Vanity

The rich, the poor, the mad and sane –
Each has a day to sigh, a day to smile
But everyone lives in that hope for a smile
And is unconscious how fast he draws near to,
Or far from, a perpetual sigh or smile.

Like a puppet we are worked into life,
Now by our left, then our right hand we are moved
Or the foot or the head as they would care.

When we think of the left hand, to the feet they'd
rather go
And we in our helplessness remain;
Living from one wish to the other and realizing not
how time flies!

As we the trick played on us
Begin to understand
And despair on our lips begin to form,
The strings of our life are cut;
Then we wonder we ever were.

A Prayer

I am not
Laying before You
The last grade of my first harvest
But what
From the simple sincerity of a youthful heart
Is the worthiest of my ability.

Whatever the nature of my offering
Bear with me,
And only accept this childish gesture

Then lay Your hands on my head
That I with confidence to maturity may grow
And thus grown should
Before You
Spread a gift more worthy of my Lord's table.

Then I also should one day glory
To tail the saintly line
Of those elders of mine who
Like subjects to their king through the ages
Have paid You their respects.
(28/11/77)

Decide the Part to Play (1)

The hills that round 'Progressive' stand
Are all in green arrayed.
Down in that well-formed basin green
In perfect white she stands

Should you from up the hill look down
A charming sight would see:
The healthy green on inexhaustible food,
The 'food' so blest in nutrients of the best;
The rays emitted by the sparkling school,
A school on seeing to which you'd die to go!

But ere, for likelihood you would,
I should in you a picture create
Of all the things of taste you'd find
In such a 'charming' home.

Jump down I say
From up your height into the midst of her!
First you would your two feet feel
Go deep in grass of green.
Their soft and healthy wind-moved leaves
Right up your knees caress.

And look around the old famed school
Its 'beauty' you must see!
Its walls meant white at places now
Of brown well-dotted be!
The panes of course of airing good

Some glass must forgo ....

The young 'pedants' . . . well they must be!
In different moods are seen.
Some grumbling are, some care-less be
But that our fun must spare.
Full-grown ones, yes, in anger be
But that to us is naught.
"Come here!" say these,
"What for?" Say those ... and on their way they go
A lovely school, a care-free one
Where naught on you is forced!
Some leaders, yes, in anger quit
That anger, who does care?
What' ere the motives they may hold
Our abode must leave intact!

But day-to-day more losses come
What must of this become?
To you my tale, in simple terms,
With all my heart entrust.
These stubborn boys, these care-free ones
What shall of them become?
You have them there, the problems all
Decide the part to play!
(Bali C.P.C 1974)

Decide the Part to Play (2)

Fellow Youth
I have a load
Weighing down my shoulders.
You have one on yours!
We have a burden on us.

This is our young, rich but fragile country.
Shall we let it drop and scatter
Into a thousand fragments?
Or shall we mould and make it more solid
Than we received of our fathers?

They their parts have done
And are giving way!
What shall we hand over to our own children?
Shall they receive from our hands
A country carefully wrought for their good
Or shall they our memory curse
For making them miserable?

Fellow Cameroonian Youth,
This is the day of decision,
This is our day:

If we want to bear the banner of development;
If we want to be national torch-bearers,
Let us note this:
Every hour judiciously spent at school as at home,
Or in other constructive daily endeavours

Is a stone for the foundation of our nation.
Let us then praise our fathers who sent us to school

Let us then know why we are here
And submit ourselves to our leaders and teachers
To mould and fashion us
The way fit for the tasks ahead.

The way is long and hard, shall we arrive?
Shall we shake off the shackles of
underdevelopment?
Let our children not live
To curse our memory!
Brethren, this is our day!
Decide the part to play!!
(Nanga-Eboko, 31/01/81, on the occasion of the 15th
Youth Day)

Be Ware

Do you know
That BLACK ANGEL is your destruction?
I saw you ever in the shadow
Of his drawn sword.
I saw you and I wept for you
But you sang, you danced, you fed
With joy
Did you sing and dance
Your end?

But he never sang, nor danced
With joy
 The BLACK BOY
He never grinned nor smiled
But for a purpose

And when you he saw at the peak of your mirth
Down came the sword!
And you and your smiles were transported …
beyond…

Blind that you are now
Tell me
Can you now his face behold?
And do you still dance and sing
As before?
(Yaounde, 01/07/78 on the occasion of the dearth of
an unruly drunk addict student)

Racial Conflicts

The angel is black
That once was whiter than white.
Black is black
And black is 'evil'
'Evil' has fallen,
The black angel has fallen,
White spears have the black flesh
Punctured

Let him bleed…! Let him bleed …!
No amount of fufu can the streams stop.
Let him bleed …! Let him bleed …!
White angel will be frightened
Then white angel will bring mortar.
But the streams will become rivers, and the rivers
oceans…
Let him bleed … !

When the oceans the lands have drowned
And there is neither ocean nor continent,
When black angel and white angel
In the blood do dissolve,
Why,
God will make Him another angel
Neither Black or White.
(Yaounde, 01/07/78: on the racial problems in South
Africa and elsewhere)

Mutual Respect

'Am very proud . . . of myself
You're also . . . of yours . . .
Let me also breathe of
The air so free …!
Eat
From the generous general earth!
Use my mouth
Vehicle to my thoughts!

Let us each dance our mortal dance
But taking care not,
Yes, forebear,
To step on each other's toes
For mere mischief,
Else we crash to the floor …
Too soon!

The Missing Link

I have a hunger
Most excruciating,
Gnawing at my inside.

Like a starving dog will on her young and kind,
I do on mine turn.
But this my appetite only heightens,
And I myself and kind only destroy.

Let me the world and beyond . . .
Possess!
Let me my stomack with all the moons and stars . . .
Stuff!
Still shall I more and more and more . . .
Need!

Strange this hunger is but to appease
Easy,
And when overlooked . . .
Deadly!

I've been looking up to my Master and Leader
Expecting He'll let me love . . .
Round some shoulder my arms would like to go . . . .
Be they black, be they white !
And feel the current flow to form a circuit
Complete!
To feel and be satisfied that
Our throbbing hearts

The same life bloods do carry.
(Yaounde, 03/08/78)

Butchering the dead

The youthful doctor
At the sight of a corpse
Is eager his theory to prove.
But naively the knife in midair
Stops . . .
Is this flesh not like mine t
And does he from my father
Differ?

The incommodious home cannot
The spirit of the poor dead
Hold!
Roaming about is it . . .
For vengeance . . . or sacrifice
Before abiding his new abode?

What if he to his old house does return
And looking up me beholds over him
Knife in hand . . .
Ready to . . . butcher?
Will I say I for his cause was
Fighting?
Or that I to his spirit was butchering him . . .
To sacrifice?
(Yaounde, 27/10/78)

Food for Thought

No!!
Let my hair be!
Do you cry out to a man
When he is about to fall into a furnace
Or when he is in . . . and turned to ash?

I say, let my tears alone!
And tell me …
Do they have to flow when the eyes are alive
And fear danger
Or when they are dead and gone?

Should we wear dark cloth in fear
Of our imminent general earthly end
Or as a plea that God should His people before time
Raise back?
(Yaounde, 27/10/78)

The Real Thing (On Death of Father)

He cried when he was born
Into this world,
And if he could tell you
You would know
He laughed
For joy on entering the next from this!
So why don't you join the others
My friend,
In laughing and celebrating
With him?

Let the goat be slaughtered!
Uncork the' bash!
Don't make it the gloomy fare-well supper
But the feasting on a new birth!

Stand up to the drums, fire the cannons!
Let it not a dearth march be
But the jubilation after a successful war!

Chant the Nfuh and let the 'Wan-Maabuh'
In its displays
Show youthfulness … vitality and virility for
A son is born to us in the next world!
(Yaounde, 27/10/78)

Philosophical

Which does a woman prefer,
To remain in a prolonged pregnancy or . . .
To embrace the acute pangs,
If any,
Of child birth and purge herself
Of agony?

And when do you suffer most . . .
When the flaming blade is directed
At your flabby masculinity or when
Unhappy days and sleepless nights are passed in
An eternal uncircumcision?
"From soil. . . to soil"
We born and are born.
Nourish and are nourished
In three stages:
The fears of the unborn child,
Who can tell?
But he plants and sucks from his umbilical cord
When no backward journey is feasible.
Then, like a snake
He surrenders to mother earth
His childhood coat and yeast-like
Begins to multiply.

Two ends of our cord of life are
Soil-ward bound:
Our umbilical cord which attaches our beings
To where we are,

Our wasted self which, gravitationally
Weighs us back home
From where we came.
But between the two stands a third:
Our manhood.
(Yaounde 1978)

Missing Facts

For how long has he been weaving
Since he started weaving
Those baskets which,
Now,
Have little advantage
In whiteness
Over his aging hair?

A basket completed
He stands up, stretches and yawns
In relief? . . . in satisfaction?
But it's lazy
That yawn and then gait
Which next carries him to his
Ancient basket store which,
Blessed in numbers by yet another,
Seems to his hair have another patch of white
Added.
How much has he achieved
By the baskets
So far,
And how much still hopes
To achieve
Before basket and hair can in colour confused be?
Or must the hair the basket out-white?
When shall the last come,
And will it a complete basket be?

How much have I read

And how much written
Since morning?
Yet I feel my energy, failing
And my brain fading…..
And what is left:
Only the desire to lie down and have a good long
rest.

When I my head from slumber raise,
Eyes shining with envy do I meet,
Seemingly saying
'If only I young again were,
To pass my time only . . .
Reading and writing,
As he does!
I've had my life woven
Into fruitless joyless years!'
(Nanga-Eboko, 24/01/78) after observing an uncle
weaving basket

Sun-set in Cameroon?

The gong at mid-day did sound and
Every heart a beat did miss.
What war, what catastrophe now
Do us befall, dear Fatherland,
At this period of time
When much of the day's work is done,
When so much of the harvest is come,
And the soul in repose
Of slumber does meditate?

Good is the harvest and the future bright,
Or is it for celebration of the promised well-being it
sounds?

"I am tired", said the cock, the king, the sun,
Being tired, rest do I reclaim, fellow countrymen"

Oh, worse than war is this!
Malediction?
The end of us all, of life should this mean~
For what life can there be
Without the sun?

But dear sun,
How presuming have we been
Never of your plight giving a thought!

What light else have we seen
Since ere our eyes the day did behold?

You the source of all life
Have been of all good.
You your light did shine
On those who in darkness fought ...
And now of peace we taste!

You pillar
Of our agricultural success
Have been on our efforts
Smiling down
Encouragingly.
Our health and education . . .
Of whom else can we think?

Your works so wonderful,
One aim did in mind have:
Our well-being and happiness.
And when we,
Or cultures and tongues diverse
Do under you unite
Of this prosperity to feast,
Would you then departure decide?

Oh, poor us!
Which would it better be,
From birth be blind
Or of sight and light to taste
Only to lose same again?

Yet others are
Who would ever faults in the sun find....

Or it's too bright or too dull;
Or it's too hot or too cold!
And when it does
To be blind, black and cold decide,
Because the sun
Tired of all this
Has for good withdrawn,
They would it were back: bright and hot.

And you say you the moon do leave behind!
How can we
Used to hotness and brightness,
To dimness and coldness return?
(Nanga-Eboko, 1982: on occasion of resignation of
1st President)

The Big Question (on millipedes copulating)

Wrapped up in this erotic ecstasy
You are immobilized
As if dead
In each other's arms!

Would that the off-springs thereof
Could thus forever from life
Such pleasure suck!

But so early in the morning,
And so much in the middle of the human path,
You lie prostrate,
Dead to the sensuality!

Could that little brain
That led you to it
No warnings give of
The impending danger
Of a foot falling . . . on you?
You know even in conscious state
Your thousand feet,
By which you are named,
Would not your life protect!

(Hours later)
There now . . . !
You had it!
Disjointed you lie

Each flattened to the ground of the midday sun,
Your life and ecstasy obliterated!
Two lives gone and generations exterminated!

Some call it wanton destruction;
Others, fate.
And yet a third: nature checking numbers!
It should be a really knowing nature indeed:
Rubbing off life, or ….
Sending man back…
Conveyed by war,
In search of his civilization
Behind the beginning
Of civilization.

Will he ever cross over again
For Nature's vicious cycle
To recommence?
(Nanga-Eboko, 26/09/80)

Hurrah to ideologies! When shall it come?

More than seven and a half 'nations'
In the small Cameroon nation,
Bustling and jostling with or for life
Like fish in a half-drained pond

Nations of all sorts . . .
Socialist, communists and, yes, capitalist . . .
And more of the –ists that can be thought of
And that have never been thought of:

Thieves and nations that steal,
Cheats and nations that exploit,
Racists and nations that discriminate,
Murderers and nations that kill,
Dictators and nations that enslave . . .

Yes, every individual is a nation,
At least potential
In miniature
With ideas and a system of government of their own.

Every nation then is represented in individuals
But not enough nations represent individual ideas!
And the 'powerful' have their ideas
Implemented at the higher nation.

I then glory in my being;
I cherish and protect it!
For should it at an untimely end arrive,

A whole nation is gone
Never to be heard of again,
Like some others in history:
Hardly born than they disappear!

No?
Then wait . . .
Till my seeds, bit by bit,
The Cameroon and Africa
Invade!
And when of my blood the circuit
The world round
Is made complete,
And every other small nation my off-spring be,
Each with the sword of justice, of equality, of love
In their hand sparkling,
Then tell me where you stand
You racialist capitalist socialist!

Why, it shall be the Promised land or
The heaven so talked of, though on earth;
A nation with one thought, one ideology
Not a nation with many nations.
(Nanga-Eboko, Sept. 1980)

Concrete Time

Young old time!
Born every second
Dead every second!

Young old Time!
Dear to bear and build up
Minutes, hours, weeks, years, centuries infinitum . . .
!
An infinite stalagmite of good old Time
Built of dead Young Time
But a colossal nothingness!
All new babes are older than Time!
Every new second, a youth to the babe
But every past one dead and gone.

If the grave of Time could open,
Let the old dead second,
If precedence it claims,
Stand up and shout:
"I am older than man!"

What is old, old Time but Man!
Still in the making . . . zero Time
As a babe, young old Time.
Back in the soil, old, old Time
Flowing in the veins of fauna and flora,
Swimming in the fishes and oceans of water!
And one day,
Back in the blood of old, old Man....

Dead but alive,
Old but young!
What is old, old time but Man?
(Nanga-Eboko, 01/01/81)

The Phoenix personified?

Man is Time and Time is Man.
Who can separate flesh from soul
Or soul from flesh?

Is there flesh because there is soul
Or soul because there is flesh?

Man is not dead and gone!
He lives in the soil and grows in the plants,
He flows with the waters and whispers in the winds.
He runs in the very blood of concrete, animate Man

He is in a blissful, 'heavenly' state
And can influence concrete, animate Man
For good or for bad
Depending on circumstances.

So sing praises to that God-image
You struggling Man!
He is the old, old young Time,
Dead but alive and growing
Young but a Methuselah!
The phoenix personified.

Small No Be Sick

I talked to my people
I pleaded with my people
But they could only shy back,
Cringing away with fright.

I said "my people
This is suicidal:
Tending your neck to be severed,
When you could some resistance offer!
And who can tell . . ."

"Yes it's suicidal" they persist,
"to face an enemy,
Mightier and stronger,
When you know
With no effort
He'll crush you!
What can a rat do before a rolling boulder?"

"It can react to defend itself.
More suicidal it is then when
In surrender,
You yourself to the enemy
Abandon!
A snake looks frail and fragile,
But does it its possibilities ignore
At the attack of a mightier foe?

Yes, my peace-loving people

Even the peaceful angels would fight back
To restore peace and orderliness.
You'll be surprised what weapons
A peaceful disciplined people embody!

Let love, peace and unity be our banner,
And justice our weapon,
Gnawing like a mouse
Secretly but courageously and intelligently
At the enemy obstacle …
To make a headway to understanding and
brotherhood!
(Nanga-Eboko, 29/06/81, on occasion of boarder
problems with Nigeria et al)

Of what use? Beauty and Desires

The eye saw
It pleased the mind.
The mouth watered!

Would the eye never saw
Nor the senses made their judgment,
And the mouth expressed its desire?
Then they cease to be eye, sense and mind!

But a judge is said to rule over all,
Instructing the eye how to see
The sense and mouth how to react!

For appreciation was beauty meant;
Goodness for desire;
Appetite for satisfaction.

But the eye coverts and commits adultery everyday,
Says the judge,
Though they must see and appreciate
Else no beauty, no goodness, no appetite, no life!

Would I could find me a good pair
Of innocent eyes,
That can see, love and desire without wrong ….
Oh, nature's poor wretched slave!
(Nanga-Eboko, 19/12/80)

More questions: What future?

I the face of the sun do see
A dirty red disc,
And the wind gently blowing feels
Chilly cold

But the afternoon I can portend,
Warmer but more dust;
Just like yesterday and days before.
Yes, this is the morning
Of a new dry-season day;
But how the dawn
Of a brand new year?

My cold hasn't abated the least;
And I slept to awake
With the problem unsolved:
How best to make ends meet!
I see a dark timeless year before me!
(Ndu, 01/01/81)

What Difference?

Her life ended with the day and year,
The old lady.
She thought of the perilous journey
Through another long twelve-month year
And decided her eyes should
The birth of that new year not perceive.

Yes, while others were
In the light of the new-day-year reveling
And wishing and hoping for a longer and more
prosperous life
Her care-freed soul in her new birth in eternity
Was reposing!
(Ndu, 01/01/81: death of a woman)

New Year Morning

Dark-bright face of the New Year dawn!
I fear your looks!
Should I greet you
With loud rejoicing,
Or should I your arrival
On my bed mourn?
Tell me!
What in store have you for me?
Tell me!
I doubt your looks!
(Ndu 01/01/81)

Communion: Old and Young

My child,
Wherever you may be,
How far away and for how long,
Nothing surpasses the necessity
Of setting your foot
Once in a while
On your ancestral soil;
Striding over your fathers' graves and
Sucking of their energy and
Bathing in their blessings;
Making them know:
However far away you may be
Your source of life they remain!

Sever the umbilical cord bringing nourishment from
the mother,
And the babe perishes;
Sever the spiritual communion between off-spring
and ancestor,
And man drifts astray
On the spanless ocean of life.
With the old, we feed and fashion the future.
(Njipnkang, 28/12/80: On communion with
grandfather)

Practically Philosophical

My child,
Can you tell me why back to earth
Things fall?
Is it because the earth more than the sky
Is larger?
No!

At the fathomless sky look
As far as the eye can see!
It stretches ----
Till the earth it seems to kiss.
Go and on yonder hill stand!
Then the sky would you see
From the earth itself seem to detach,
And into the abysmal abode withdraw,
No obstacle to the eye leaving!

Yes!
In fear of this 'void' it is,
For identity, protection and comfort,
Do we fall back to this mother-abode of us all,
Where from our body came and belongs!
(Njipnkang, 28/12/81: from more communions with
grand-dad)

Part II: Many Hearts, Many Voices

by

Judith Kome Ngantu

My Redeemer

I Sing a new song,
Sweet smiling, sweet whistling,
Your love is heavenly,
Radiating a peace unknown
For you are deeping down white hands,
Into my bag of trash,
Cleaning up my smeared face,
Oh My Redeemer.
Your love refreshes my spirit,
In a way only it can do,
And brings with it Your peace,
A gift no trauma can undo.

How can a Sovereign One,
Be Creator and friend to creature,
Be Father to be born Son to mankind,
Be life yet die for the dead.

Your mystery is endless and yet,
We know enough to dwell in You,
Your love is everlasting and there,
We find assurance and learn to love like You,
Oh my Redeemer.

My Baby

I could hold you like this forever,
My golden egg in cotton sheets,
Fragrance of innocence and fresh milk,
A delight to see, a warmth to feel.

I could waltz with you like this forever,
Dancing to the music that is you with you,
Like soul mates known before creation`s dawn,
We bind; we glide till the forty winks come.

Your eyes in mine,
Mine in yours outshines,
All the world`s calamities,
And I hope again,
I dream again,
Of joy complete,
I hold your tiny feet,
And see tomorrow's gift.

I can sing to you like this forever,
Soothing every pain, every day
Saying it won't always be okay
And life could be full of delays.

But I will pray for you forever,
In tears, in joy, in fever,
Till knees are bent and tender
And sleeping is forever.

Queen of the Night

I dread the dawn I see,
Red clouds of sun rays,
 That comes with bills to pay,
Anger on the landlord`s face,
Bitter wives full of hate,
Again, the dawn is coming with disgrace.

I watch you rest in peace,
Enjoying the sheets of today`s lover,
You`ve paid the bill like all your brothers,
Rocked my hips like there is no other,
With dawn you will remember,
That you are a father,
A husband to a holy mother.

Yet tonight all will come and all will leave,
The dusk will bring forth new tragedies,
New laughters, drinks and same follies,
And strength is renewed for new sins,
I spray the perfume and spread fresh sheets,
And wait for the change left after drinks,
Praying ceaselessly for the dark anointing,
Of cold beer and heavy hot drinks,
To blow your minds and make you seek,
The heat of hell's sanctuary,
Then I will receive you like royalty,
For night has come and made me queen.

The Widow

You make me smile in my days of darkness,
And then I laugh when the sun is in my nest,
I try to dwell in this sphere of redemption,
With nothing but hopes for more than action,
You could be the one,
But if you are what was he, the clouds?
That come and go as whether changes,
Only faithful to their destinies,
He said the same words like you,
You and I together for good,
But he changed his mind and death he chose,
My sons and I were lost like fools,
Now tell me the truth my suitor,
Who loves a six times mother widow,
Is it the left overs of my youth you seek?
Is it a companion to carry your wreath?
Is this madness real?
 Is it a dream, or the dream,
Of a lonely woman still hungry to feel?
Smile still,
Make me laugh still,
Since I still live,
We could end up united amiss and in bliss.

Desperation

He didn't like that she was short,
She didn't like the way he walked,
He smiled too much,
She never did at all,
It had to work out anyway,
Time had put them in this tiny hallway.
The little lines around her eyes,
Were dark like the night,
Fifty was around the corner,
But in his pocket no dime nor dollar.
Tim had been too fat,
Brown too far,
Michael too loud,
Jesus was the answer.
He had woken up at forty,
Behold, long gone was puberty,
No job, no wife, no babies,
He ran to the church for mercy.
They needed each other,
For worse, if not better,
Nothing could separate them,
Desperation was beyond the fear of hell.

Love Lessons

Linger on my beloved,
Take your time and do the wooing,
I will take mine and do the denying,
For that is what mama taught me.
Sing the songs my beloved,
Cut the flowers and drop on my doorstep,
Write the letters and sneak through the crooked
bend,
Whistle at my window, no, throw the pebbles,
I will pretend I didn't like your letters,
I will ask you to let me be,
Flinch, like you itch my skin,
Show that I'm a decent lady,
For grandma taught me so.
Then when I finally say yes,
You will take me to the Riverside,
Give me a surprised picnic,
Touch my chick, and probably more,
And with each picnic is a fading in your eyes,
Anxiety gradually shifting to familiarity,
Then new letters you will write,
New flowers you will bring,
But not to my doorstep,
For your daddy taught you so.

You once were mine

You once were mine,
When my chest defied gravity,
When my eyes knew no lies,
Your darkness was my light,
In your eyes was me,
A better version of me,
A version I believed,
With you I could fulfill.
You once were mine,
When I became yours,
Fitting in your thighs,
In a holy fight,
In an ordained norm,
Wrestling till dawn,
Snubbing the sun,
Till babies were born.
Still you claim to be mine
But you crave the youthful touch,
Of waspy waists and yellow thighs,
Of honey lips and eyes of fire,
For the sun we snubbed,
Left us with a black dusk,
I cry, I weep but I won't mourn,
For before your love, there was His Love.

Dilemma

Under my feet is the earth,
Full of life, full of death,
We laugh at our tears,
And enjoy our fears,
Who knows tomorrow's sorrows?
For today seems to know no hope,
Who will make the right prayers?
Whose lips are moist enough for words so tender?
Who cares for the Earth's tears?
Who will dare the devil without fear?
Who lives to love, and loves not only to live?
In this dreamy world full of greed,
Where smiles are for the lazy lions,
And the ribs of strong hyenas dry in the sun,
Wash your hands let's bite the bit,
And quench at least the fire in our bellies.

The Sermon

Sing songs of praise,
And watch the car come,
Shout out hallelujah,
And move into a villa,
Sow your seeds of gratitude,
Your pastor loves the tune,
All is well for the chosen ones,
It's sowing time, says the Word,
Dance like David, sacrifice like Solomon,
For a hundred sacrifices bring a million returns,
To who will believe and empty the purse,
If it's from another's purse bring still,
If it's for the children's soup bring still,
If it's profit from the midnight clients bring still,
For on the alter all is sanctified,
Bring and it shall be multiplied,
Like the endless flow of oil,
That filled up the jugs like soil,
Poor are the ignorant,
Aren't you tired of being the servant,
We are born to reign,
For our God is sovereign,
Bring forth your tithes and offerings,
And watch how you become king.

Life

Life is a waste, like a fresh flower on a harlot's hair,
It is a mystery, like the moon that courts the earth,
Going round and round,
knowing no way out,
It is sweet like cold spring water in scotching heat,
That oozes out like heaven's gift,
You breathe in the life you see,
You fight for the life you wish,
Whatever you choose,
Love it,
And live it,
And let not life live you,
Or leave you.

Again

When he does it again
Shed the tears Again
Cry to die again
Kneel at your feet again
Promise not to sin again
Ignite the fire again
Grow the hope again
Build the bridge again
Bring the dreams again
Hail you louder than before
Treat you better than before
Raise you higher than before
To drop you deeper than before
Much deeper than before
Much deeper again.

It hurts at night

It only hurts at night,
When I run out of the strength to fight,
Pushing down what memory highlights,
The pain, that cuts through the soul like Satan's
knife.

It only hurts when I lie,
When I long for sleep and it denies,
Then I run short of strength to fly,
To keep dwelling in the realm of lies.

I only cry in the dark,
To remain suspended like Noah's Ark,
No one sees where the tears land,
I drown in questions that have no answers,
Why me? Why again? How do I flee from this trap?

I only sleep in the morn,
When the early birds sing songs,
Of hidden hope that comes with the sun,
Promising that all isn't well but you can fake some
more,
In the light, no one sees the smile that mourns,
A silly joke, a little laughter and the trick is done,
To keep me staggering to the next nightfall.

Woman-man

I didn't have them,
But only I felt the weight of the absence,
No one saw my longing,
The envious eyes that followed pompous tips,
That danced proudly on mounts,
With music or without a sound,
The bulging blouses,
The bumpy skirts.
My cravings had a different meaning,
I longed not to have like the others, but to own.
How could I explain,
That there was a mistake,
That my lashes were too short for my liking,
That my feet were too big and I wanted heels,
What will my father's rough black hands do to me?
When I wore the hair and borrowed a lipstick,
Where will mother hide in shame,
After viewing a man like image of herself,
Should I reach out and embrace the nightmare?
No! I will make it my nightmare,
And break not fragile hearts,
With the dreams of a young man,
With a crying, no, a dying soul of a woman.

Cassanova

Beneath the smile, is a thousand miles, away from love,
The charming eyes hide debts of profound deception,
The sweet words are songs from the snakes parted tongue,
The packaging is the offer, the empty parcel,
Beneath is the emptiness and heartlessness of a pathetic soul,
A condemned evil nature, only less than Christ's redemption,
A power to destroy, every notion of innocence,
To abuse, everything sacred,
Every creature that still believes in love,
And desires a taste of the adventure.

Red Eyes

Beneath the rage of the sun,
Under the massive rusted metallic tray,
The scorching steel stings the tender numb fingers,
The neck moves to the acquired stability rhythm,
Supporting the tiny head that carries Fako mountain,
Red eyes with a thousand tears never shed,
Wonder desperately searching,
A feeble voice struggles out for a desperate
attention,
With a breath uneven,
Tiny iron calves strain forth to unknown destinations,
With cracked heels in shredded plastic shoes,
Some answer the call for necessity,
Others do for mercy,
For they know that in the sun's anger like in the
heaven' s tears,
This little child will slave in and out of time,
To sell every crap for mama's smile,
So red eyes follow with sorrow,
The size and age mates that glow,
The bright uniforms and white socks that follow,
Into great buildings where knowledge was said to
overflow,
 Services mama can't pay for, nor borrow,
But the garbage on the rusty tray is to be sold,
So, she wonders off the no cross zone,
Like an adult with every pain in control.

Mama

You scold and again you nurture,
You dread my decisions for the future,
No passion is greater than your dream of seeing me mature,
enduring the experiences of life's torture.
Your voice echoes even from your grave,
Reminding me of all I should evade,
The dangers of life and your own mistakes,
The pain that should not come my way,
 Tears never to be shed again.

Your voice is forever in my mind,
Sweet like a toddler's rhyme,
Soothing like a lullaby,
Even from where you lie,
Your sacrifices tell no lies,
Today I stand tall and again I shine,
Radiating the love and confidence you brought alive
In this once timid heart of mine.

Beauty Technology

What if I added a hump on my hip?
The pants could better fit,
Doctor fill under my tits,
I have the right cloth to get it popping,
We now have a choice don't we?
If your man's eyes wonder on that which is big,
Buy your own and keep his eyes on it,
If your lips are a little too thin,
Pump it up and add the grease,
Cook the skin, rub the njansa, make it less swarthy,
let it bleach,
Add the hair like the lashes,
Who cares as long as it makes you happy?
Do it for you, for the glamour or for him,
Anything and everything is sweet,
As long as it takes not away your peace,
Nor your sleep,
Nor your identity.

Virtues

The heart that bleeds unseen,
When even in darkness the shadows flee,
Toughens like the turtles shelf,
With cracks that tightly blend,
And visible scars unend.

The tongue that echoes silence,
When even in innocence receives a sentence,
Musters control Like a loyal army,
That keeps calm in the heart of the battlefield.

The feet that runs to rescue,
When even the helpless is the source of bad fortune,
Grows in strength like the heels of the horse,
That runs a thousand races showing off.

For when the heart like the tongue and the body
yield to your authority
The power of fate is made minimal,
And life's cancer can be answered.

My African Man

My black gladiator in the darkest arena,
Seeks not the acclamation of a blood thirsty crowd,
But a decent meal, clothes and home,
First for the baby and the mummy.

My black champion carries not heavy swords,
But heavy duties of building a home from a barren
society,
Battered not by a better adversary than limitations,
Raising arms of diligence to crush hunger's evil eye.

My black wrestler uproots the fangs of
disillusionment,
Beheads the economic monsters,
Tames the consuming fire of recklessness,
In endless faces of trial.

My black hero is no fiction,
My black star is famous in my heart,
My black saviour's stories are in my diaries,
Worthy of sweet praises,
From me, his hailing black woman.

My flower pot

In my heart's flower pot is a mighty sunflower
But beneath sprouts plants I didn't plant,
Some are creepy, and creep down maliciously,
 not in a hurry to find the sun,
Some hide in the shadows of the wide yellow petals,
Minding not the challenge,
No complaints,
And then the climbers,
Wrapping their necks and waists
around the huge sunflower stalk,
Hanging on like a leech.
I feed one but all is nurtured,
The gleam of the host gradually darkens,
 Sucked up by unwanted guests,
I try to weed off the unwanted,
But the soil is not tender,
Ripping one could off root the other,
Then comes the Water of life,
The earth is moistened,
Enough for frail roots to be pulled out,
And for strong roots to regain strength and stand
taller.

No Promises

I promised you nothing,
Remember, no pact,
No swearing to secrecy,
So I brag,
Of my money making man.

No promises,
Promises are for happy ending Seekers,
Struggling to master fate, to be keepers,
Reaching out to consciences long withered,
Holding on to the mirage of a lover.

The sunlight has this power,
Turns werewolves to husbands and fathers,
Well if our escapades get to your mate,
Remember this madness started with your desire,
To quench a devilish midnight fire.

Good women

A good woman is a desired nightmare,
Wants to be treasured like Helen of troy,
A faithful woman is difficult to please,
Building standards to caress the moon.
A caring woman doesn't just care,
She cares and expects triple in return,
A sweet woman awaits unending gratitude,
Whether you are or aren't in the mood,
So tell me why you yet desperately,
Seek these kind of women.

Proverbs

Mock the gods for my stupidity,
My proverbs are mine,
Not the Divine.
Love fate for your success,
It loved you more than the worthy and best,
Chew your agony with the right frown,
Don't keep a smile as you drown,
Fix not the face of a shattered heart,
Sick optimism evades reality,
Sham and shame are the world's greatest recipe,
You can be the cook or the consumer,
Escape not to fight another deadly battle, just flee,
For only you know you, can understand you than
yours, than me.

A Pastor's tears

I mourn not for the dead,
But for the doomed eternal lifeless,
And the still walking dead.

I cry not out of sorrow,
But pain in reaching out,
To skeptic hearts hardened by vanity to the core.

I rejoice not in wealth,
But in the light that shines on the hill,
In the ever-burning candle,
Of souls gone and here,
Journeying proudly with their Lover.

We age

Like the sheep in the fields,
Grazing till the day of slaughter.
We age,
Like the chicken that feed,
Lays and waits for Christmas.
We age,
Like the Island that kisses,
And cajoles the waves, till the day of rage.
We age,
And sway like trees,
Till civilization presents its needs.
We age,
Not like Abraham and Isaac,
With centuries on their sleeves.
We age,
Or age we wish,
And only can wish.

Vanity

Beyond the dreams we dream are dreams that
should not be dreamt,
Dreams that grandpa and grandma called sacrilege,
Beyond our desperate needs are needs that should
not be met,
Needs that we don't take to the alter of Light,
Beyond our battles are fights that should not be
fought,
Some victories are more costly than worthy,
Beyond our dreams are needs that we fight for,
Which are simply not worth our peace.

Tears of a Bastard

So, you are dying
When will you love me?
Years unending waiting to be seen
So, you are leaving?
When will you teach me?
Mend me, groom me, train me
Show me the way father.
So what did I do to be born outside?
Did I start the game that led to me?
So how different am I from the ones inside?
I look more like you.
So when will you hold my hand and lead me to
school,
When will you carry me on your shoulders?
When will you love me oh father,
Now that Our Father calls for you?

www.ingramcontent.com/pod-product-compliance
Lightning Source LLC
Chambersburg PA
CBHW060315050426
42449CB00028B/2076